THROUGH THE LOOKING GLASS AND BACK

Your Passport to Identity

Susan G. Bondow and Paul Kelm

SELF-IMAGE

NORTHWESTERN PUBLISHING HOUSE
Milwaukee, Wisconsin

Library of Congress Card 93-84288
Northwestern Publishing House
1250 N. 113th St., Milwaukee, WI 53226-3284
© 1993 by Northwestern Publishing House.
Published 1993
Printed in the United States of America
ISBN 0-8100-0489-5

Contents

In her more than fifteen years as a professional counselor, Susan Bondow has seen countless examples of what sin has done to self-image and of how Christ is the answer. She holds a Master of Social Work and has a private practice, The Family Therapy Center in Appleton, Wisconsin. Susan frequently writes and speaks on popular Christian counseling topics.

Serving now as a Campus Pastor at Wisconsin Lutheran College in Milwaukee, Wisconsin, Paul Kelm draws on a wealth of experience in communicating the gospel of Jesus Christ. He has also served as a mission pastor, a campus pastor at the University of Wisconsin, an administrator for the Commission on Evangelism, a consultant to churches, a Spiritual Renewal Project Director, an author, and a speaker.

Editor's Preface

Christians in Crisis Series

At some time in our lives, everyone of us faces a crisis. We wonder who we are, what we are doing, what's happening to us, why we face certain problems. Many crises come and go, and we get through them with relative ease. Others flood into our lives and threaten our well-being—lingering, smothering, overwhelming.

This series of books addresses such potentially destructive crises in a Christian's life and offers God's help to the Christian in crisis. You will learn from these books how God's law and gospel apply to each crisis. You will see how God's Word can help you in your most critical need.

To ensure the integrity and the practical value of this series, each volume has the combined wisdom of a writing team with both theological and scientific training, usually a pastor and a psychologist. All the writers are Christians, who look first to the Scriptures for their guidance.

Northwestern Publishing House offers these little books to you as sources to help you understand and even as tools to help fix what is bothering you. We caution you, however, that they are not meant to offer you an exhaustive treatment to be used in place of personal counseling. Where crisis patterns persist, we urge you to seek counseling from professionals in the field.

Finally, we present this series with the prayer that all your crises may be restored to calm in Christ.

"Come to me, all you who are weary and burdened, and I will give you rest. Take my yoke upon you and learn from me, for I am gentle and humble in heart, and you will find rest for your souls" (Matthew 11:28).

Gary P. Baumler

Preface

Self-esteem has been touted as the key to health, happiness, and success. Building self-esteem, therefore, has become a psycho-social industry attached like a parasite to education and counseling, business and religion. Countless people are seeking self-esteem. Relatively few appear to have found it.

But why don't people like themselves? Why do they question their worth, wear masks, create images, engage in self-destructive behavior? Why are some people searching for their identity while others are running from it? The radical conclusion is that, deep down, there really IS something wrong with us. Denying it or trying to surmount it won't work. Confronting it and answering it will.

In this book you will find applied psychology to help you understand what you may be doing to yourself. In this book you will find clear theology to help you understand why self is so distorted and what God has done about that. In this book you will find yourself.

Guilt is what sin does to our view of self in relationship to God. Jesus Christ died for sin to reconcile us to God and take away that guilt. Shame is what sin does to our view of self in relationship to others. Jesus Christ rose from death to assure us that we have his righteousness and his identity. In this book you'll find Jesus, the answer to the guilt and shame that have robbed you of a right view of yourself.

"I have been crucified with Christ and I no longer live, but Christ lives in me. The life I live in the body, I live by faith in the Son of God, who loved me and gave himself for me. I do not set aside the grace of God, for if righteousness could be gained through the law, Christ died for nothing." (Galatians 2:20-21)

CHAPTER 1

Masks in the Mirror ～～～～

We spend much time trying to put together the pieces of our identity. We look to our past, to our heritage. We all remember familiar tales we enjoyed as children, passed on from generation to generation—filled with as much fiction as truth. We trace our family trees, searching for roots, identity, connection. We rehearse family joys and tragedies. We whisper well-kept family secrets.

We look to others—parents, teachers, peers—to affirm our budding identities. Sometimes we are nourished, sometimes destroyed.

The image in the mirror becomes clouded. Who am I? We play roles; we wear masks—masks composed of layers of cover-ups and deceptions that we tell ourselves about ourselves in order to like ourselves.

We use masks to try to convince God (and ourselves) that he should recognize us as his own children once more. We use masks to bypass God altogether, convincing ourselves that we can attain perfect wholeness ourselves, and have our own identities, separate from him. We wear masks for others, to gain acceptance, a sense of belonging, and happiness by pretending to be what we are not.

We are, perhaps, like Lisa or Dick or Kara or Fred. . . .

The court case

As we look in on Lisa, Dick, Kara, and Fred, they are about to begin the most important day in their lives. Each has received a summons to appear in court. The charges include suspicions of wearing false identities, hiding behind masks, and posing as imposters. The nature of disguise was said to fall into two main categories: self-inflation and self-deflation. Each individual has been ordered to stand before the judge and give an account of his or her identity. Their very lives hang in the balance.

The sun slid over the horizon, the dawning of a new day, the day of her court appearance. Lisa stood before the bathroom mirror. It was time to get ready. She reached for her brush and began to untangle her long, dark hair. As she gazed into the mirror, tears welled up in her large, brown eyes. "I'm no good. . . . I'm just a failure," she thought. "What identity do I have to defend? I'm just an insignificant nobody, a hopeless case, another number in the file."

Abused as a child, she sought affirmation and love in unhealthy relationships. Time after time, she was victimized, rejected, and abandoned. Alone and caring for two children, she was overwhelmed by life. How could she face the task ahead? She sighed, her small frame seemingly caving in on itself, as the tears streamed freely down her face.

Dick nervously whistled a tune as he reached for his tie. Standing before the mirror, he made final adjustments and stepped back for inspection. He nodded with approval at the figure in the mirror.

"Yes, Dick, old boy," he mused, "you've got to pull this off. The group is counting on you as an example of perfection, positive mind control, and tapping into your unlimited potential. Just walk into that courtroom and show them who

They are to establish their identities and prove themselves worthy of existing.

you are. You have the power within you to make it happen, don't you?"

Dick wished that he felt as positive as he sounded. He had been wrestling with this identity issue for a long time. It had all started when he signed up for a class in "Connecting with Your Higher Self." Promises of getting in touch with your own inner strengths sounded appealing at a time when he was feeling stressed-out and unproductive. The class had led to continued participation in a group made up of other searching individuals. At first, Dick felt accepted and affirmed. But lately there seemed to be more comparing and competing. Others seemed to be progressing toward perfection. He told them of his successes, too. Yet, down inside, he knew that reality wasn't as rosy as he portrayed it. This court appearance would polish it off for him— a tribute to his worth, connection to all that is great, and an elevation in status, power, and position.

Pushing any doubts aside, he squared up his shoulders, grabbed his brief case, and headed out the door.

Kara was right on schedule, clothes neatly laid out, every detail of her preparation carried out with orderly precision. She glanced in the mirror and was greeted by the image of a tall, austere woman, business-like, direct. She smiled, not a gushy, beaming smile, but one of control and refinement. "I am set," she said to herself. "My case has been carefully prepared. I have done my best, and expect the recognition and reward that I deserve."

The alarm pierced the silence. Jolted to consciousness, Fred groped to shut it off. The effort left his head pounding as he sank back into his pillow. "My court appearance. . . . ten-o'clock A.M. . . . this morning!" Reality hit like a lead brick. He stumbled out of bed and into the bathroom. As he peered at his reflection in the mirror, the consequences of the previous night's drinking binge met him face to face. "So much for a send-off to claim my place among the masses," he reflected. "Oh, well, nothing a shower, a cigarette, and a nice, stiff drink can't cure."

Standing before a judge in defense of our identity is not a pleasant situation to contemplate. It smacks of comparison, criticism, judgment, possible rejection. Put yourself into that situation. What do you see in the mirror? Are you Lisa, Dick, Kara, Fred? Who are you?

You may feel defensive and angry, yet anxious and fearful. Your identity is on trial. Your heart pounds, your palms sweat, and your mouth goes dry. You run your defense through your mind a thousand times, over and over—making corrections, strengthening arguments, trying to get it just right. Who am I supposed to be? Where are the holes and contradictions in my case? How can I present my strengths and cover up my weaknesses?"

Masks—our many faces

We have different ways of dealing with such a challenge. We check out our appearance in the mirror and try on different masks and cover-ups for size. We have our favorites.

Some of us prefer large, heavy, majestic masks. These masks carry much responsibility, are often intimidating to others, and command deference and respect. Our identity becomes hidden in issues of power, authority, over-responsibility, and control.

The role of "Supermom" is a good example. Hidden responsibilities incorporated under this singular title include those of caretaker, babysitter, nurse, teacher, disciplinarian, social director, housekeeper, cook, taxi driver—all of which must be carried out to perfection with love, patience, kindness, and self-control. Somehow, we expect to earn our reconnection to God or to someone whose approval we crave.

Others prefer smaller, simpler masks, often shriveled and worn, tear-stained and fragile. Expectations of us, from others and ourselves, remain low or non-existent. Big eyes stare out from scared faces as we try desperately to blend into the woodwork. "Oh, I couldn't possibly do that. I have no talent. Surely someone else would do a better job."

Masks can be fierce and threatening or compliant and apologetic. We pull out plastic smiles that cover up our hurts and pains. Couples, taking their familiar seats in church each Sunday, return home for another week of fighting, arguing, or silent withdrawal. Our routine physical reveals a suspicious lump. We worry secretly and alone. The car breaks down, adding another burden to the already strained budget. We manage to look so good from the outside. Who would ever guess what lies within?

We hide behind self-pity, wallowing in failures, disappointments, hurts. With each encounter of defiance and disrespect, we despair of being a good parent. We receive a poor grade on a term paper and rationalize, "Who needs school? Might as well quit."

Our "calm, cool, and collected" mask hides our vulnerabilities, our feelings. "So I didn't get the job. No big deal. I didn't want it anyway."

We pretend that hurtful words or teasing don't phase us. We're tough; we can take it. We wear an armor. We dare others to get close.

A "positive thinking" mask can provide a temporary motivational boost. But when we ignore the facts of human weakness, failure, inadequacy, and vulnerability, we set ourselves up to be disappointed in ourselves and others. "Why do I keep making the same mistakes? Why can't I be happy all the time? Why can't you always be there for me? Why don't you change so that our relationship can be perfect?"

When the realities of life become too painful, we can escape into addictive masks, covered by the mood-altering effects of alcohol or drugs. We look to chemicals to make us whole, to fill in the gaps. "Alcohol makes me more outgoing, more sociable."

"I can communicate better with others. I feel more connected."

"When I'm high, nothing matters anymore. I can forget the pain."

We even play games of tearing down others' masks to build up our own. One man is openly critical of another for physically abusing his wife and walks away feeling superior. Arriving home, he is oblivious to the verbal battering that comes out of his own mouth.

A father and son work together on a project. The son comes up with an alternate way of completing it. Since the father feels that he must always know more than his son, he rejects the son's idea.

<u>Our masks become protective walls</u>. They provide a fantasy of who we are, a refuge from the pain of reality. Pereta Elkins Dov, in her book, *Glad to Be Me,* has described our condition in this way:

Don't be fooled by me. Don't be fooled by the face I wear. I wear a mask. I wear a thousand masks—masks that I am afraid to take off; and none of them are me.

Our masks become protective walls. They provide a fantasy of who we are, a refuge from the pain of reality.

Pretending is an art that is second nature to me, but don't be fooled. For my sake, don't be fooled. I give the impression that I am secure, that all is sunny and unruffled within me as well as without; that confidence is my name and coolness my game, that the water is calm and I am in command; and that I need no one. But don't believe me, please. My surface may seem smooth, but my surface is my mask, my ever-varying and ever-concealing mask.

Beneath lies no smugness, no complacence. Beneath dwells the real me in confusion, in fear, in aloneness. But I hide that. I don't want anybody to know it. I panic at the thought of my weakness and fear being exposed. That's why I frantically create a mask to hide behind—a nonchalant, sophisticated facade—to help me pretend, to shield me from the glance that knows. . . .

Who am I, you may wonder. I am someone you know very well. I am every man you meet. I am every woman you meet. I am every child you meet. I am right in front of you. . . .

Masks—our response to shame

Why do we need masks? What is it we are hiding from? What is there about our identity that we try so desperately to avoid it?

(Shame.) It touches the core of our being and is the most painful, helpless, and lonely feeling we experience. It makes us want to run and hide. It is something we are all familiar with. It first touched mankind in the Garden of Eden and has been with us ever since.

Merle A. Fossum and Marilyn J. Mason, in their book, *Facing Shame*, define shame as "an inner sense of being completely diminished or insufficient as a person. It is the self judging the self. A moment of shame may be humiliation so painful or an indignity so profound that one feels one has been robbed of her or

Shame. It touches the core of our being and is the most painful, helpless, and lonely feeling we experience.

his dignity or exposed as basically inadequate, bad, or worthy of rejection. A pervasive sense of shame is the ongoing premise that one is fundamentally bad, inadequate, defective, unworthy, or not fully valid as a human being."

Is it any wonder that we want to run and hide, or find protective coverings to shield us from our imperfections?

The wait outside the courtroom seemed unending. People shifted restlessly, stood, paced, and sat down again. At last the heavy, wooden door swung open. All attention immediately went to the small figure in the doorway. "We're taking a one-hour break for lunch. Everyone is expected back promptly by one o'clock this afternoon."

The message was swallowed by the sudden outburst of chatter. Lisa wondered how she would pass the time when a rough voice said, "Care to join us? We're going to the cafe across the street for a bite to eat."

Lisa found herself nodding an agreement. She grabbed her purse and followed the others.

Once seated, they gave each other brief introductions. She learned that the man with the rough voice was Fred; a woman named Kara seemed polite but distant; and the gentleman with the bold, vivid tie was Dick.

All of them made sociable conversation throughout the meal, but it wasn't until they were finished that Lisa hesitantly stated, "I don't know how I'm going to pull this off."

"Someone told me how it all started," interjected Fred. "People wanted to be something more than what they were. They were tempted to believe they could be like God. In wanting to be more than they were created to be, they became less."

"They lost it all for us," stated Kara wryly. "Now we're all trying to make up for it, to get it right once more, to become what we ought to be."

"I've tried. I can't," sighed Lisa. "How I wish things would go back to what they're supposed to be."

Sensing the negative tone of the conversation, Dick jumped in. "Hey, why limit yourself? I'm not giving up. We can be our own gods. We don't need God."

"That may be OK for you, but I find the Man Upstairs to be pretty scary," said Fred, looking down at his hands. "When I look at what I've done with my life, I don't see him greeting me with open arms. I don't know what to do so he will like me."

"That's right," said Lisa. "I can never be acceptable to God. All I deserve is his punishment, or worse, his rejection."

"It does present a dilemma, one that I am trying to face head on," intellectualized Kara. "I strive for perfection in all I do, and, compared to others, I think I live a very good life."

"That doesn't work for me," said Fred. "How do we undo the past? How do we end the shame?"

"I've heard that God has a plan," said Lisa softly.

"God's plan?" the others echoed.

Suddenly the small group bustled with activity. "We can't go back to him, not after all this time, not to face the shame," said Kara as she picked up her tab.

Dick reached for his coat, "Besides, now we have our pride—our masks, our cover-ups."

"We would have to give them up, and return in utter humility, just as we are," said Fred, putting out his cigarette.

"Yes, of course. You're right," said Lisa as she slowly rose from the table. "This we can not do."

Masks went up, guards returned, walls were erected as everyone pulled back into him- or herself and returned to the Court House.

Pride, despair, and our internal core of shame keep us self-centered. We, who once were so focused on God that we did not notice our own nakedness, are now totally engrossed in ourselves. We have to be. How else can we stay on top of the web of lies, the masks, the false selves, the defenses, the walls, the distancing, the protection that we weave around us?

In the end, we lose. We lose our re-connection to God, which re-connects us to our selves, which re-connects us to others, which re-connects us to life and circumstances. "You will not surely die," said the serpent, and we believed him. We became the living dead.

Deep inside, we feel lost and alone, empty and afraid, no matter how we may appear on the surface. We all have little child-like eyes that peek out from behind our protective walls, out from under our protective masks—longing, yearning, yet trapped by the walls of pride, despair, and shame.

Look at the people and situations depicted in this book. See yourself written in these pages, and identify with the human dilemma we all face. Perhaps you have been struggling for a long time with solutions offered by the world. Perhaps you have been trying to find self-worth through positions of power, job advancement, authority, and control. Perhaps you pride yourself on your personal appearance, social graces, and popularity. Or do you bury yourself in self-gratification, lusts, and momentary pleasures without accountability? Perhaps you consider yourself above such behaviors and look down your nose at others in self-righteous judgment.

Whatever mask or cover-up you are currently hiding behind, it is all part of an unending struggle that is empty and unfulfilling. There is only one answer, one solution to man's dilemma. It is God's solution. I pray that as you read, you will dare to look at the one who is the truth, for, indeed, the truth will set you free.

REFLECTIONS

1. Are you willing to look into the biblical mirror of the law and see yourself as you are apart from God?

2. Are you conscious of sin in your life?

3. Are you willing to face your actual self in all of its humiliation and shame?

4. Are you willing to say that you are capable of the vilest of thoughts; the most cutting, piercing, and demeaning

words; and the most heinous of acts against self, others, and God?

5. Can you honestly say, "What a wretched being I am! Who will rescue me from this body of death?"

CHAPTER 2

The Exchange— God's Image for a Mirror

" 'Let us make man in our image, in our likeness. and let them rule over the fish of the sea and the birds of the air, over the livestock, over all the earth, and over all the creatures that move along the ground.' . . . The man and his wife were both naked, and they felt no shame" (Genesis 1:26; 2:25).

Reflecting God's image—no need for a mirror

The problem of identity goes back to the first sin. Picture Eve sitting on a rock, basking in the sun, hair gently blowing in the soft breeze. She is unruffled, happy, appreciative of all the beauty surrounding her. Tender whisperings of love and gratitude flow continuously to her Lord.*

> She slid from the rock and sauntered toward the edge of the pond. The soft, smooth sand cradled her feet and gushed between her toes. Oblivious to her reflection in the mirror-like surface of the water, Eve carried the clear image of her Lord. Unaware of her nakedness, she was clothed in the knowledge of God. She knew her identity and her purpose; she knew her

---

*Editor's note: This account of Eve is not meant to fill in details of how she fell to Satan, but it is an imaginative way to show what the fall did to her sense of identity, made ugly and imperfect by the sin that separated her from God.

limitations. She was not God. She was made in his image, and her limitations did not shame her.

Leaving the water, she strode down the path toward the garden. She could see Adam in the distance and hurried to meet him.

She knew her identity and her purpose.

What a relationship they had! It was filled with love, laughter, and selflessness.

Eve loved the time that she spent with Adam. But nothing could compare to the Lord's visits. He WAS love, unconditional acceptance. Always listening, teaching, challenging, he encouraged them to discover more of him and his creation.

Satan's temptation: offering the "mirror"

Early the next morning Eve hurried to her garden plot. Adam was already there, tilling a fresh patch of soil. She could envision the flowers, faces reaching toward the sun, and the juicy fruits that her garden would bear. Kneeling, she dug her hands into the warm, rich earth. Smells of nature filled her nostrils. Eve worked steadily, unaware of her silent visitor.

The great deceiver, having clothed himself as a serpent, watched her every move. He was prepared for this encounter with an attack, a denial, and a claim. Slowly he slithered forward.

Reaching for a clump of dirt, Eve detected the subtle form of the snake. "Such a lovely spot you have for a garden," he hissed in greeting.

Sitting back on her heels. Eve surveyed her work. "Why, thank you," she said. Adam ceased his work and came closer to listen.

The crafty serpent twined around the trunk of a newly planted tree. "Did God really say, 'You must not eat from any tree in the garden'?" he challenged, attacking God's Word. He enjoyed shifting the focus from all the blessings that were hers to the one thing that she was denied.

"We may eat fruit from the trees in the garden," responded Eve, feeling strangely uncomfortable. "But God did say, 'You must not eat fruit from the tree that is in the middle of the garden, and you must not touch it, or you will die.'"

The serpent was pleased. He caught Eve's addition to the Word, about not touching the tree. His challenge was working. He pushed on with denial, a blatant rejection of what God had declared. "You will not surely die," the serpent said to the woman.

Eve felt confused. Her mind seemed cloudy, a feeling she had never experienced, and one she could not seem to shake.

Aware of her struggle, the serpent coiled for the final blow. He made his claim, "For God knows that when you eat of it your eyes will be opened, and you will be like God, knowing good and evil."

Her eyes left God and turned to self.

What did this mean? Was her Creator withholding from her, hindering her from reaching her full potential? Could she be like God himself?

Strange feelings flooded her body. She was pulled by a gnawing feeling of incompleteness. An incessant tugging suggested some pleasure to be experienced. There was also a distant sense that a still, small voice was calling her name.

Shift in focus: exchanging God's image for man's

She closed her eyes. Her focus wavered. She found herself drawn toward the forbidden tree.

She made a choice. Her eyes left God and turned to self. She plucked the fruit and took a bite. She stared at the fruit in her hand and, turning to Adam, who was with her, gave it to him. He took it and ate also. Instantly they were alienated from God and stripped of his image. Their eyes opened to a different world, and they realized they were naked. They felt shame.

Unbearable reflection: naked and ashamed

Eve raced to the pond, the serpent's laughter echoing in her ears. Tearing through the brush, she burst into the water. Slowly the waves and ripples subsided until she was face to face with her mirror image. She gasped. Never has mankind seen such a clear, accurate reflection of humanity apart from God. The reflection was unbearable.

The beginning of all cover-ups, masks, and false identities

One misdirected focus on self severed us from God. One look at the consequence shamed us to the core. That look marked the beginning of all our masks and cover-ups, the beginning of our hiding from God, from ourselves, from one another.

The sinful image of man is now inherited, generation after generation. It remains an unbearable reflection. From within and without, we are bombarded with shame.

Our protection lies in our masks. We learn the family masks. We learn the family rules. We discover the roles available in the family system and which ones we can, or are expected, to fill.

The masks of family roles

In her book, *Another Chance,* Sharon Wegscheider identifies five basic roles played out in most families. These roles include the Enabler, the Hero, the Scapegoat, the Lost Child, and the Mascot.

Enablers carry a heavy load. They are loyal and over-responsible, covering up for others, usually a spouse, protecting them from the consequences of their behavior. They cope by making most of the decisions, playing both mother and father to the children,

From within and without, we are bombarded with shame.

controlling the finances, making the necessary excuses, and staying on top of the chaos. Not only do they grow weary in the process, but they prevent the very crisis that could bring about change. We might imagine "in-control" Kara filling this role.

What about the Hero? The Hero provides the family with hope for success. Heroes are achievers who must perform in the outside world and be a source of pride to the family. When they are not performing well, they feel empty and worthless. Dick was one who felt he needed to be the Hero.

Scapegoats offer the reverse image of the Hero. Unable to compete with the Heroes, they withdraw from the family and look to peers for a sense of belonging and acceptance. Eventually they may turn to chemical escape. Starving for attention, they act out frustrations and bring disgrace to the family. With real family problems denied or kept secret, the Scapegoat is often blamed for any family dysfunction. They bear labels such as Problem Child, Troublemaker, or Black Sheep of the family. Fred, awaking with his hangover, was exhibiting the behavior of a Scapegoat.

The Lost Child enters a chaotic scene. Sensing the tension and drama already in play, he adapts by getting lost, being a loner, and staying out of everyone's way. Social skills remain underdeveloped, expectations are low, and a sense of specialness and worth is missing. Poor, abused Lisa fits this description.

Mascots reap big rewards for laughing, clowning, and playing practical jokes. They get positive attention for their antics and relieve the seriousness and strain in the family. The art of being funny can manipulate and control situations, but the drawback comes when others don't take them seriously. Immature, out of touch with feelings, and unable to be quiet or intimate, the Mascot continues in a reckless pursuit of attention. Fred is the one most likely also to fill this role.

In addition to the family roles, we observe the family values and beliefs—acceptable behavior for men, women, adults, children; attitudes toward sexuality, finances, religion, relationships, intimacy. We learn our entitlements, withholdings, expectations, goals—everything needed to equip us to pass on the mirror, and to pass on the masks. We take on family identities, but we increasingly struggle to find our own identities.

We take on family identities, but we increasingly struggle to find our own identities.

Dick glanced impatiently at his watch. It was almost 5 o'clock, and his name had not been called. To make matters worse, the waiting area, instead of emptying, was becoming more crowded. He pulled out his handkerchief and wiped his brow. "Does the whole world need to claim its worth, or what?" he thought to himself.

His attention was suddenly stirred by three men walking briskly toward the front of the room. Upon clearing his throat, one of the men addressed the group.

"We apologize for the delays, but, as you can see, the proceedings are taking longer than anticipated. To expedite matters, we will begin tomorrow by working in groups designed to assist you in evaluating your case."

He went on to explain how each group would make a "Journey to Grandma's Attic" with the purpose of identifying generational patterns of dealing with shame and their effects on individual identity.

Dick's response was mixed. He was disgruntled over the loss of a day, and the additional time demand. But part of him was intrigued—rummaging through trunks, reliving old memories, perhaps connecting with a lost piece of identity or uncovering a family secret!

The next morning arrived. Cars began to pull into the old Victorian farmhouse. Group #3 would make their "Journey to Grandma 's Attic" here. A back stairway gave them direct access to the large, third-floor attic.

Kara briskly mounted the stairs. Her eyes swept the room. It was just as she had imagined. She observed clutter, nostalgia, racks of clothing, hats galore, trunks, furniture —truly an antique lover's paradise. People were already exploring, poking in trunks, trying on clothes, rocking in rocking chairs, and looking through old photograph albums. People remembering, re-living, re-thinking.

She spotted Fred, standing mesmerized in front of a large, antique dressing mirror. As he stared at his reflection, his gaze was returned by that of a young boy around the age of seven. He had learned early the tricks of covering-up and secrecy.

He remembered the pain of scrutinizing eyes—parents, siblings, aunts, uncles, peers. Their eyes, like microscopes, had probed and magnified every detail of his being in search of flaws. He sought escape from the criticism, teasing, and hurtful comments that had poked at his core of shame. Rebellion, smoking, drinking, defiance became his release. If they thought that he was so worthless, he might as well act the part.

Kara turned her attention to a small group gathering by the attic window. They were discussing childhood be- haviors, child- hood needs— needs that had been shamed, especially if they made a parent uncom- fortable, em- barrassed, or they didn't live up to per- fectionistic or adult stan- dards. Kara caught a few comments.

If they
thought that
he was so
worthless,
he might
as well act
the part

"I was too full of energy. Settle down, sit still, and be quiet were the messages that I always heard."

"It wasn't OK to want things, or to need help. We were taught to be tough, never to need or want anything from anyone."

"I remember the stumbling attempts I made at new activities. Being the youngest, there was always someone around who could do the activity better. I pretended that I didn't want to play, but what I really didn't want was to be laughed at."

"I don't remember being a child, or having a childhood. In our family, we had to grow up fast."

Kara's focus drifted to a heavy, unkempt woman busily trying on hats. At last she found one that seemed to please her. It was a colorful spring hat with a large plume trailing off to one side. Kara noticed the sparkle in the woman's eyes. "That's a very becoming hat," she ventured to say. The woman turned, her face lighting up with pleasure. "Oh, thank you," she said. "I'm having so much fun." She paused. "I feel a little selfish. I'm so used to taking care of everyone else that I feel guilty being here by myself and having fun to boot." She laughed and turned back to her reflection in the mirror.

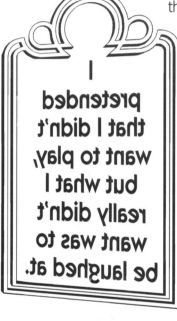

I pretended that I didn't want to play, but what I really didn't want was to be laughed at.

Kara picked up an old photograph album and slowly leafed through its pages. "What secrets do you hold inside?" she wondered. She studied the faces. "Oh, I know that you can't talk about such things—addictions or mental illness, unwanted pregnancies, bankruptcies, scandal, deaths, accidents, anything with a glimmer of shame to it." Kara leaned back and closed her eyes. She thought about her own family. She thought about the undefined cloud that always hung in the air. There were no words, no breeze, to blow away or break up the storm. "So you ran, and worked, and struggled to get out from under it. You had to be perfect, flawless, controlled. Perhaps if you could achieve enough you could rescue the family from the cloud." What was her relationship to God, and how did so many barriers get in the way of seeing it clearly?

The inflation/deflation cycle

Sometimes it helps to return in memory to our childhood to understand better our identity problems as adults. In fact, we should be aware that we haven't necessarily left childhood as far behind as we think.

As adults we have grown up physically. We walk, talk, and look like adults. But within each of us is a little child with unmet needs, a child that is searching to be special, important, acceptable, and loved. In relationships, we expect others to take care of and parent us. We are disappointed when they don't. The challenge is how to get close to someone when our identities are covered by masks and disguises. How can you be close, when inside you feel flawed and imperfect?

Within each of us is a little child with unmet needs, a child that is searching to be special, important, acceptable, and loved.

The child within instigates our compulsive/addictive behaviors. Responding to the child in us, we try to be things we cannot be, or else we settle for being less than we can be. Often we vacillate between the two. These behaviors inflate or deflate our identities. Through these false identities we seek to find a solution to our human dilemma.

More than Possible
(Inflation)

Superachiever
Hero
Righteous
Powerful
Grandiose
Proud
Perfect
Critical
Responsible
Driven

Less than Possible
(Deflation)

Underachiever
Scapegoat
Wretched
Pathetic
Self-pitying
Pseudo-humble
Worthless
Mascot
Irresponsible
Lost child

The inflation/ deflation cycle

Breaking the cycle

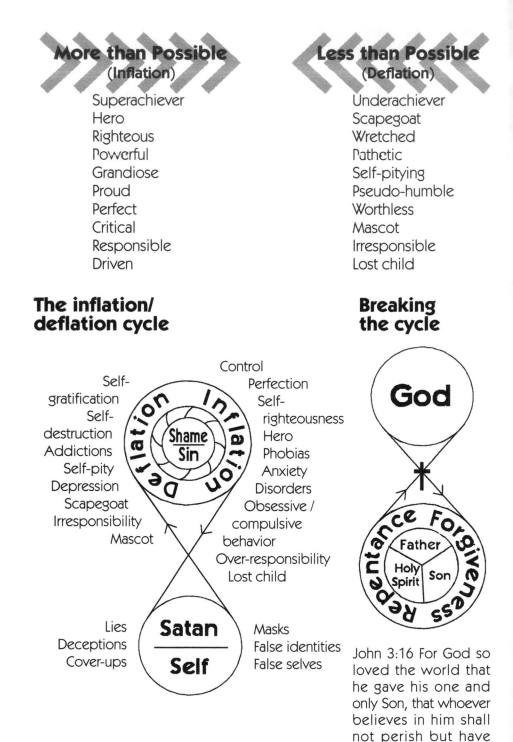

John 3:16 For God so loved the world that he gave his one and only Son, that whoever believes in him shall not perish but have eternal life.

Spinning around a core of shame, behavior patterns of inflation and deflation shape our identities. In the inflation phase, we try to be more than we can be, and in the deflation phase, we are less. We can continue through life, spinning in endless circles that are always empty and unfulfilling.

Paul writes, "What a wretched man I am! Who will rescue me from this body of death?" (Romans 7:24).

Reflections

1. Can you recognize the roles of Enabler, Hero, Scapegoat, Lost Child, and Mascot in your family of origin?

2. What role(s) did you play? What role(s) do you still play today? Are you more likely to inflate your identity or deflate it?

3. Were childhood behaviors or needs shamed in your family of origin? If so, which ones?

4. Do you recognize masks, addictions, patterns being handed down to you from generation to generation? If so, what masks, addictions, or patterns do you see?

5. What discoveries would you make in a "Journey to Grandma's Attic"?

Roles: men, women, adults, children

Attitudes toward: religion, money, sexuality, expectations, entitlements

6. How have these attitudes, roles, and masks shaped your identity?

CHAPTER 3

Distorted Images —The Art of Disguise Inflation

"Come one, come all. Step right up and enter the Fun House. See yourself instantly transformed. What reflection do you want to be? Fun for one and all. Step right up."

Most of us have experienced the inside of a "Fun House" or "House of Mirrors." Following a maze of twists and turns, we are confronted unexpectedly by our distorted reflections—stretched, crunched, magnified, deflated.

Concave, convex, and plane mirrors

Different shapes of mirrors cause the distortions. Concave mirrors are hollow and curved like part of the inner surface of a sphere. These mirrors are magnifiers and inflate our reflections. We appear larger than we are.

Convex mirrors have the opposite effect. Curved like part of the outer surface of a sphere, they form images that are demagnified. We are deflated and appear smaller than we are.

Only when we stand in front of a plane mirror, a looking-glass mirror, do we see an accurate reflection. Light bounces off us, passes through the glass, and hits the shiny layer behind the glass. Then it bounces straight back. We see ourselves as we really are. These are the mirrors we avoid.

Concave mirrors—inflated images

"Step right up and peer into our concave mirrors. See yourself as more than you are. Step into the image of perfection."

Wouldn't it be wonderful to be perfect? No more mistakes. No more blame, no more shame. Perfect relationships—no more misunderstandings, miscommunication, or unresolved conflicts.

With such bliss serving as the ever-dangling carrot, is there any wonder why we strive for perfection—or at least to be more perfect than those around us?

**Wouldn't
it be
wonderful
to be perfect?
No more
mistakes.
No more blame,
no more shame.**

In her book, *Overcoming Perfectionism,* Ann Smith defines perfectionism as "a compulsive pattern of behavior and thought aimed at compensating for low self-esteem, repressed emotional pain, fears of abandonment and shame." She says, "It is those feelings that we're trying to overcome with this crazy, perfectionistic-looking good behavior."

Control is essential. Anything that is not controlled is risky. We feel vulnerable and exposed.

So say good-bye to spontaneity, creativity, fun, frivolousness, and relaxation.

Feel the coils winding tighter and tighter, adding tension, strain, anxiety, stress. We watch, poised—ready to spring, pounce, destroy anything that threatens our mask of perfection.

Court was adjourned for the day. They had been given a reprieve from the tension surrounding the hearings. In addition, everyone received free passes to a nearby amusement park for some light-hearted fun.

Dick sauntered into the park. He walked past vendors busily preparing for the day ahead. The air was filled with the smells of food, animals, grease, and sweat.

"Welcome to the House of Mirrors," beckoned a smiling gentleman, resplendent in tuxedo and top hat.

"Thank you," responded Dick. He entered the brightly painted doors.

Expecting to be greeted by shimmering reflections, Dick stopped abruptly. Instead of facing mirrors, he faced a warning posted in bright red letters:

For your safety, we advise strict adherence to the following rules when looking into the mirrors of magnification.

1. Don't feel or talk about feelings.
2. Don't think.
3. Don't identify, talk about, or solve problems.
4. Don't be who you are—be good, right, strong, perfect.
5. Don't be selfish—take care of others and neglect yourself.
6. Don't have fun. Don't be silly or enjoy life.
7. Don't trust other people or yourself.
8. Don't be vulnerable.
9. Don't be direct.
10. Don't get close to people.
11. Don't grow, change, or in any way rock the boat.*

"Somehow these rules sound familiar," thought Dick. He slowly proceeded through the dimly-lit corridor. He came to a door. He opened it and went in. A black-and-white-clad troupe descended upon him.

"Come in, come in," they chattered.

"Allow us to prepare you for the concave mirrors of perfection."

"We teach the art of disguising yourself as more than you are."

"We'll build on your strengths. . . ."

---

*Robert Subby, and John Friel, "Co-Dependency —A Paradoxical Dependency," quoted in *Co-Dependency, an Emerging Issue* [Hollywood, Fla: Health Communications, Inc, 1984], 31-44)

"Disguise your weaknesses. . . ."

"Get set for the P's of perfection."

"Position, Power, Possessions, and apPearance," they all shouted together.

Dick blinked, struggling to get his bearings. The bright lights and walls of mirrors momentarily blinded him. Meanwhile, his hosts were not idle. They placed a large cap upon his head and, armed with a wide assortment of feathers, looked at him expectantly.

"What feathers are in your cap?"

"What are your position, your titles, your degrees?"

"What organizations, boards, committees do you serve on?"

As he answered, they tucked feathers into his cap. Surprisingly, the cap began to feel rather heavy. He was then given a large tray to hold in each hand.

"How powerful are your positions?"

"Over whom do you have control?"

"How much authority do you carry?"

For each response, a delicate china teacup was placed on the tray. "Do not let them fall," he was warned.

Others were busily fitting him into a new suit of clothes. "This will be perfect for you."

"Clothes make the man."

"Conceal, reveal, accentuate the positive."

"Now for the inflated attitudes.

"How is it possible to live up to this image?" he wondered.

We have a large selection. Arrogant, intimidating, controlled, distant, critical, patronizing . . ."

"Excellent," reported his hosts upon completion. They spun him in front of a looking glass. Dick stared in disbelief. It was he all right. But what polish, what style!

A momentary wave of fear shuddered through his body. "How is it possible to live up to this image?" he wondered. But there was no time for contemplation.

"You are now ready for the corridor of mirrors," explained one of the group. "Be sure and carry your trays proud and high. Juggling your image and its responsibilities takes cleverness and skill."

Dick was ushered out of the room, with the door closing soundly behind him. He breathed a sigh of relief. A perfectionist disguise is a lot of work. He surveyed his surroundings. A twisting hallway lay before him lined with magnificent, majestic mirrors. Raising his trays high, he began his journey. He admired his reflection and stifled the thought that his outsides didn't match his insides. "Think positively. You can fill this image," he said to himself.

On approaching a tall, narrow mirror, Dick was startled to find that it did not contain his reflection. Instead, a young man returned his gaze. The youth spoke, "Do not dare to put yourself in new situations or relationships where you are at risk of making mistakes." Recognition struck him. It was his cousin, John. The cousin who avoided eating in crowded restaurants, waiting in check out lines, or riding in crowded elevators. Such exposure brought on panic attacks.

Dick hurriedly moved on. He was feeling the weight of the trays. Uncle Bob appeared in another mirror. "Do not dare attempt new behaviors or patterns of relating to others lest they come across poorly, and you embarrass or humiliate yourself." "How fitting," thought Dick. Uncle Bob would be the last person to apologize or admit a mistake, much less tell anyone that he cared.

After several twists and turns, Janet Demmer, an old schoolmate, saluted him. "Do not dare open yourself up to new areas of learning, or your ignorance may be revealed, and you will be found wanting." He thought back to her dropping out of school and wondered if there was a connection.

Dick was intrigued. He picked up his pace. Rounding a corner, he came face to face with his father. "Do not dare to pursue close, intimate relationships that provide an opportunity for someone to see beyond your walls and through your masks," resounded the familiar, gruff voice. Dick felt sick, weak, numb. His father lived in a distant fortress. How he hated those walls!

His brother caught his eye, peering soberly from a mirror. "Do not dare to make a mistake. You must be perfect, or you will lose control." It was then that Dick's knees buckled. He felt himself slipping, falling, unable to maintain control. The clattering of trays and shattering of teacups echoed down the hall.

"Do not dare to make a mistake. You must be perfect, or you will lose control."

A tremendous amount of energy is expended in maintaining control. In attempting to do so, we face an impossible task. We become weary and burdened. We also become angry, disappointed, resentful, bitter, and frustrated. We end up despairing of everyone because we have insisted on humanity being what humanity can never be—perfect. We look to man to be what only God can be. We set ourselves up to be constantly disappointed, let down, abandoned, betrayed.

St. Paul writes, "What a wretched man I am! Who will rescue me from this body of death?" (Romans 7:24).

Reflections

1. What are the feathers in your cap upon which you base your identity? (Personality, appearance, power, position, possessions, etc.)

2. What were the rules in your family of origin? Which ones still hold your loyalty? What changes would you like to make?

3. What do you avoid in your life because of fears of mistakes and imperfections?

4. Imagine taking off the burdens and responsibilities of being perfect. How would you feel? What would you like to do?

CHAPTER 4

Distorted Images —The Art of Disguise Deflation

Convex mirrors—deflated images

"Step right up and peer into our convex mirrors. See yourself as less than you are. Step into the IMAGE of despair."

The masks of control and perfection have come crashing down. The burden was too great—one failure too many, rejection, disappointment, mistakes, responsibility, rule. Despair sets in. "I give up."

"I quit."

"I can't do anything right, so why try?"

"If you can't keep the rules, might as well break them."

"I'm too worthless even for God to salvage."

> Fear of making mistakes is replaced by the belief that I am a mistake.

We swing to the opposite extreme, that of self-deprecation. Fear of making mistakes is replaced by the belief that I am a mistake.

We wallow in self-pity and decide that since nobody else seems to care, neither will we. Why not smoke three packs of cigarettes a day, abuse alcohol or drugs, engage in immoral sexual activities, over-eat, over-exercise, over-spend?

These activities can give us a momentary high, a brief instant of feeling special, important, acceptable, and loved. We continue to seek these brief moments, compulsively abusing ourselves in countless ways, or abusing others physically, sexually, or emotionally.

Lisa was pleased to accept Fred's offer to go to the amusement park together. They arrived in the early afternoon. The park was hot, dusty, and bustling with people. After waiting in long lines and being jostled by the crowd, they decided to look for a cool, quiet spot.

"Enough of phony perfection. Stop striving for the impossible," hollered a disheveled man as they passed by. He shook his cane at the crowd. "Why fail at measuring up, when you can measure down? Enter the land of the convex mirror, the land of self-deflation."

Lisa grabbed Fred's arm. "Why, it's the House of Mirrors! How about going in?" she asked.

"It's gotta beat the heat," said Fred.

The old man smiled a toothless welcome. The cool dampness of the building embraced them immediately. "What a relief," sighed Lisa.

Fred stared up at what appeared to be a written warning. He brushed off some of the dust, but the red lettering underneath was faded and worn, making it illegible. Someone had scribbled over the sign the words "Rules were made to be broken." "I wonder what message we're missing here?" said Fred.

Lisa, however, had wandered down the hall. Fred found her around the corner facing a closed door. "Shall we?" she asked.

"By all means," he replied, opening the door.

Flawed mirrors—irresponsibility

A scrawny, bearded man jumped to his feet. "How do? Pete's the name," he said. "You folks are just in time to try out some of my new mirrors. Found this one down at the junk yard just yesterday," he said proudly.

Lisa and Fred exchanged glances. The room was dimly lit, untidy, and full of cobwebs. It was also filled with mirrors— shattered mirrors, broken mirrors, cracked mirrors, mirrors with flaws, spots, and distortions.

"Do you have any mirrors without flaws?" asked Lisa.

"Oh, no," the man said, shaking his head. "I don't like the responsibility. Gave it up long ago. I'll stick with the mirrors in the Wing of Irresponsibility." He pointed to the right.

I don't
like the
responsibility.
Gave it up
long ago.

Heading in that direction, they found that the room opened into an expansive wing. Mirrors were scattered in all directions, free-standing mirrors, hand mirrors, mirrors on the walls, mirrors from the ceiling. Mirrors with obvious flaws marring the reflections. "Go ahead, take a look in the mirrors," Pete prompted.

They cautiously approached a tall, thin mirror. They were stunned to see their distorted reflections fade. In their place was the scene of a mother and her teenage son.

"You missed your orthodontist's appointment again? That makes ten in a row. What am I going to do with you?" The scene slowly disappeared.

Lisa hurried to an oval-shaped mirror. She became entranced by a phone conversation between a school principal and a worried mother. "John did not show up for school again today." She could identify with the mother's sense of frustration and hopelessness.

Fred was also involved in the reflection of a phone conversation. This one was between an irate boss and his employee. "You were due into work forty-five minutes ago. Where in the world were you?" He could easily imagine himself in that situation, mumbling excuses, promising it wouldn't happen again! Praying that he wouldn't lose his job.

Fred and Lisa both approached a wide mirror suspended from the ceiling. A woman appeared sitting in the squalor of a home obviously in need of cleaning. "Keep the noise down, kids. . . . I can't hear the TV."

A small hand mirror offered the reflection of a young man opening his mail. He carelessly tossed several new bills onto a mound of unpaid ones. A friend waited for him at the door. "Time to go party, pal," he said to the friend. "How much money do you have on you for tonight?"

"Some of these sure hit home for me," said Fred. He felt an added weight on his shoulders. "I thought they might," grinned Pete. "Care to see another wing?" They hesitated, then agreed.

Cracked mirrors—self-destruction

He led them around to a back hall and turned the corner.

"Cracked mirrors," indicated Pete. "This is the chamber of self-gratification, also known as self-destruction." Lisa and Fred moved uneasily among the mirrors.

Brushing some cobwebs aside, they eased up to a mirror. A large woman was studying the shelves of the refrigerator. "Mistakes at work, failing my classes, no friends, no fun. I need something to eat. "

Another mirror showed a man shuffling into the bar and sliding into his old, familiar seat. The bartender sauntered over, a smirk on his face. "Thought you'd be back. Have a beer on the house. Drown your troubles." Fred felt a little weak.

"Let's try this one," said Lisa steering Fred away from the painful image. The mirror revealed a group of teens huddled together, waiting for their turn with the needle. "Can't wait to shoot up." "Can't wait for the high." "Nothing else matters except the high."

They turned to leave the chamber but stumbled into a plain, rectangular mirror nailed to a pillar. A man stared back at them as he slicked back his hair and poured on his aftershave. "Gonna look good tonight. See if I can find some action. Maybe pick somebody up. No messy relationships for me—just a simple one-night stand, thank you."

"This is the chamber of self-gratification also known as self-destruction."

By now, both Fred and Lisa were moving slowly. "Everything feels heavy," noted Lisa. Fred slumped into a worn wicker chair. "Things sure look different in these mirrors," he said. "Behaviors that I thought were cool and easy are looking shallow and empty. I never realized that irresponsibility and self-gratification carried so much weight."

"I was confused when you linked self-gratification with self-destruction," said Lisa, addressing Pete. "Now I understand what you meant."

Broken mirrors—Self-pity

"This way, this way," said Pete helping Fred out of the chair. "There is another spot to visit." He escorted them past the work room for mirror repair, and out into a front alcove. The small chamber was lined with broken mirrors. "This area is devoted to self-pity," Pete said.

Lisa felt her heart flutter. She knew these disguises well. She stood timidly before a mirror. Two women came into view engaged in a conversational game of "Who Has It Worse?"

"My daughter got a speeding ticket last night."

"Oh, yeah ? Well, my son is in jail."

"My husband doesn't love me anymore."

"Oh, yeah? Well, my husband is dead."

"Nobody likes me."

"Oh, yeah? Well, everybody hates me."

Lisa turned away. "I think they'd go on forever," she said.

"That's right," said Pete. "Try another mirror."

Fred was observing a different battle. A man was surrounded by a hovering group. Throughout the conversation, the man would secretly peek out to make sure of their concern. "Oh, woe is me. I'm no good," he wailed.

"Behaviors that I thought were cool and easy are looking shallow and empty."

"Oh, yes, you are," retorted the group.

"Oh, no, I'm not. I can't do anything."

"Oh, yes, you can."

"Oh, no, I can't. I'll never make it."

"Oh, yes, you will."

"Oh, no, I won't."

"It sounds like a broken record. I can't believe how annoying it is to listen to that, and yet, I've done the same thing myself," said

Fred. He walked over to join Lisa, who was engrossed in a scene. A woman in the midst of tears, sobbing into a mound of kleenex, was crying out.

"I need someone to rescue me. I need someone to take care of me. I need someone to pay attention to me. I need someone to make me feel special and important." She paused to reach for another tissue. "I do everything for everyone, and not one word of thanks. I'm a door mat, taken for granted. All I do for everyone else and nobody cares about me." Lisa had tears in her eyes as she turned from the mirror. Fred put his arm around her shoulder. "We all feel like that sometimes," he said.

"Yes," said Lisa, "but I can see how I use self-pity to manipulate others and gain attention, too."

Shattered mirrors—depression, despair

Pete informed them that there was only one studio left. "Care to join me?" he asked. "I'm afraid it's too late to turn back now," said Fred. Lisa agreed.

Pete led them down a long hall. They passed through a door and into a tunnel that gradually angled downward. They walked a long way in silence. The air became heavier, filled with a chilling dampness. The tunnel narrowed. An arched entrance finally appeared in the distance. A faint, shadowy sign above the opening read, "Trapped in the Snare of Despair."

Lisa cringed. What a foreboding introduction. Pete noticed her hesitation. "There are mirrors inside," he said. "Come and see."

They entered the room together. It was surprisingly barren. There were only a few mirrors along the outside walls. Mirrors that, like broken dreams, had been shattered —sharp edges but dulled emotions.

They stepped before a fragmented mirror. Only a broken silhouette appeared. "Depression. Too heavy to move. I just want to close my eyes and sleep my life away. Nothing matters," echoed a female voice.

They moved on to another mirror, another silhouette. "Worthless. I've let everyone down. I am rejected, abandoned, alone, and scared. It is all I deserve."

Lisa trembled, and again they moved on. A profile of a man, head in hands, emerged. "Not respected by my wife, distanced from my children, fired from my job—what's left? Might as well end it all."

Pete spoke, "Trapped. Trapped in the mirrors of self-reflection. Nowhere to turn. Having hit bottom, unable to reach out. There seems to be only despair and hopelessness."

"Is there any hope, any hope, any hope . . . ?" echoed their voices through the tunnel.

"God," said Lisa softly.

Reflections

1. Are you trapped by irresponsibility?

   In what areas of your life are you irresponsible, refuse to be accountable for your behavior, and place the blame on others?

2. Are you trapped by self-gratification/self-destruction?

   In what ways are you seeking self-gratification? How is this self-gratification destructive to yourself, your values and beliefs, and to others?

3. Are you trapped by self-pity?

   List your favorite versions of "Woe is me."

   How is Satan deceiving you into focusing on what you don't have rather than seeing the blessings that you do have?

4. Are you trapped by despair?

What is weighing you down?

What tends to bring about feelings of depression, worthlessness, and despair?

Is there any hope?

CHAPTER 5

The Looking Glass— Return To Humiliation ~~~~~~

Is there any hope?

We hope in ourselves. We hope in other people. We hope in power, position, and possessions. We fill in the gaps with alcohol, drugs, and other addictions. Or we give up hope and fall into depression and despair.

Denial: Barrier to plane mirror honesty

We are in denial, spiritual denial—denial of our imperfection, denial of our need for forgiveness, denial of our emptiness apart from God, and denial of our deep-seated longing to find peace and reconciliation with God.

Hazelden Foundation offers some helpful definitions: (from *Dealing With Denial, #6 in the Caring Community Series,* copyright 1975, by Hazelden Foundation, Center City, MN. Reprinted by permission.)

1. Denial is a psychological mechanism or process by which human beings protect themselves from something threatening to them by blocking knowledge of that thing from their awareness.
2. The denial that this thing exists in their lives is below the level of awareness. It is done subconsciously. In other words, the person doesn't know or is unwilling to admit that it exists.

3. The problems overshadow or cloud a person's ability to realize or recognize that the thing, set of circumstances, events or phenomenon are actually happening in their lives.
4. It impairs judgment and results in self-delusion, which locks the individual into an increasingly destructive pattern of living. [Note: We are defining this pattern of living as the Inflation/Deflation Cycle, spinning around the core of shame.]
5. This process of denial has many faces which may manifest or characterize themselves in any one or more of the following ways:
   a. Simple denial—maintaining that something is not so which is indeed a fact and very obvious to important others in the person's life.
   b. Minimizing—admitting superficially to the problem but not admitting that it is serious in scope.
   c. Blaming (also called projection)—denying responsibility for certain behavior and fixing the blame on someone or something else.
   d. Rationalizing—offering alibis, excuses, justifications, or other explanations for behavior. The behavior is not denied but an inaccurate explanation of its cause is given.
   e. Intellectualizing—avoiding emotional, personal awareness of a problem by dealing with it on a level of generalization, intellectual analysis, or theorizing.
   f. Diversion—changing the subject to avoid discussion of the topic that is threatening.
   g. Hostility—becoming angry or irritable when reference is made to the problem causing conflict. This is a defense to back the challenger off the problem.
6. Denial is automatic—it operates below the level of awareness. The affected individual does not really know that he/she is engaging in the acts of denial.
7. Denial is progressive—the affected individual sets up such an elaborate system of denial mechanisms that

they pervade the entire personality and become so enmeshed that they are extremely difficult to penetrate.

Sin and its consequences—our loss of holiness and perfection, and our resulting separation from God—are the real problems with mankind. We are steeped in denial about accountability to God and our inability to control our own destiny.

Denial is a tool of Satan to keep us focused on ourselves and this world. Denial and secrecy—sweeping problems, failures, and imperfections under the rug—these keep us from reality, honesty, and healing, just as they keep dysfunctional family members stuck in their dysfunction.

Denial is a tool of Satan to keep us focused on ourselves and this world.

Rapha, in its 12-step programs for co-dependency and chemical dependency, summarizes the many lies that Satan tells us with the following four false beliefs:

False beliefs	Consequences of false beliefs
I must meet certain standards in order to feel good about myself.	The fear of failure; perfectionism; being driven to succeed; manipulating others to achieve success; withdrawing from healthy risks.

False beliefs		Consequences of false beliefs
I must have the approval of certain others to feel good about myself.	→	The fear of rejection; attempting to please others at any cost; being overly sensitive to criticism; withdrawing from others to avoid disapproval.
Those who fail (including me) are unworthy of love and deserve to be punished. [There is no alternative.]	→	The fear of punishment; propensity to punish others; blaming self and others for personal failure; withdrawing from God and fellow believers; being driven to avoid punishment.
I am what I am. I cannot change. I am hopeless.	→	Feelings of shame, hopelessness, apathy, inferiority; passivity; loss of creativity; isolation, withdrawing from others. *

Plane mirrors: The biblical mirror of the law

God gave us his holy law so that we become conscious of sin. It is his tool to free us from false beliefs, denial, masks, and cover-ups. It is a tool to bring the truth to light, to get rid of the secrets and the hiding, to face reality.

But we misuse the law. Denial's many faces come out to protect and defend us from the truth. We may do this in several ways.

We misuse the law as a "scale of self-worth." This allows us to be selectively self-righteous. "Look at all the good things I've done this week: I went to church, attended Bible class, visited

---

*McGee, Robert S., Springle, Pat, and Joiner, Susan, *Rapha's Twelve-Step Program for Overcoming Chemical Dependency,* Rapha Publishing / Word Inc., Houston and Dallas, Texas, 1990. Reprinted by permission.

Aunt Agnes in the nursing home, waited hand and foot on my family, took over for the fumbling civic committee, and rescued my niece from some bad decisions."

We justify ourselves as doing more good than bad, or at least coming out even. "I'm holding my own. I've done some good, done some bad. At least I must warrant a '5.'"

We make comparisons and find fault with others in an effort to make ourselves look good. "OK, so I've had a bad week. But you should see John, and Mike, and Jeff. They're worse off than me. When I look at them, I'm not that bad."

Oswald Chambers once wrote: "The great enemy of the life of faith in God is not sin, but the good which is not good enough. The good is always the enemy of the best."

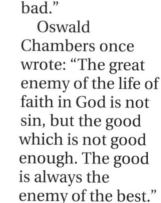

We misuse the law as a "scale of self-worth."

Another misuse of the law makes it a driver or motivator. To be worth anything, we must do everything and do it perfectly. Performance is our emphasis. The goal of our life becomes perfection, held out before us as the ever-elusive carrot on a stick. We are unable to appreciate life as growth and progress, not perfection, . . . unable to accept either our failure at perfection or God's gift of perfection.

Here we find the hero, competing, striving, achieving—in a joyless battle to attain worth.

A third misuse of the law is as a self-punishing tool, beating ourselves up with it for not being better. We become immobilized by guilt, hopeless and despairing. Instead of being led to confession, we hide all the more under self-deprecating, self-defeating, and self-destructive behavior. We get caught in the "If Only Syndrome."

"If only I were a better person."

"If only I had tried harder."

"If only I hadn't said this or had said that."

"If only I had more talent."

"If only I had a different family background."

More barriers to plane mirror honesty

You may be at a major crossroads at this point. You can identify with all the struggles and burdens that we face in trying to control our own destiny. But the idea of taking an honest look at YOURSELF may raise many barriers. Those barriers are not put there by God but are a result of sin:

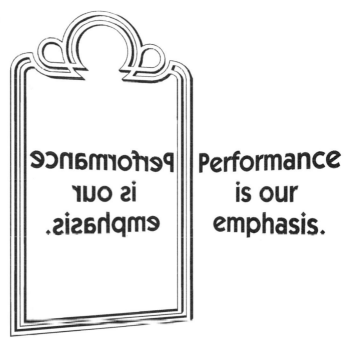

Performance is our emphasis.

1. Having been hurt, disappointed, betrayed or abandoned by those closest to us, we may be afraid of becoming close to God and risking further hurt and abandonment.
2. If "religion" in a hypocritical form is forced upon us, we may rebel by refusing to be involved with the real God, unwilling to separate his truth from the religious "show" demonstrated for us by others.
3. In punishing, abusive families, where love is conditionally dispensed, we may transfer those human

shortcomings to God, viewing him as shaming, blaming, judging, and rejecting.

4. Our core of shame itself may shut out God's message of salvation.

5. Our inflation phase, filled with self-will, self-righteousness, and pride, may blind us to our need for God and to the lies inherent in the idea of being gods ourselves.

6. In the deflation phase, where self-will denies God's willingness or ability to save us, we may allow our own despair and groveling, to keep us from approaching God in his Word.

7. Underneath all of our excuses is the self-will that refuses to be humbled before our holy and almighty God.

Underneath all of our excuses is the self-will that refuses to be humbled before our holy and almighty God.

8. Behind our self-will, which acts in disobedience to God, is Satan, the father of lies who desires to

keep us turned from God,

keep us focused on ourselves,

keep us convinced that we can be gods ourselves so that we will never seek the true God, and

keep us from God's gift of salvation, his solution to our human dilemma, through Jesus Christ our Lord.

The large wooden doors of the court room opened. Lisa, Fred, Kara, and Dick waited anxiously. The sound of their names pierced their consciousness. It was time. Slowly they went through the motions of gathering belongings and moving through the masses toward the open doors. Hearts pounding, adrenaline flowing, they stood before the judge.

"Let me hear your accounts," demanded the judge, seated on a raised platform behind a massive, ornately-carved desk. The court reporter waited expectantly.

Dick stepped forward. "I am at one with all that is. I am enough. I find what I need inside myself. I am whole. I am complete. I am perfect just as I am right now," Dick shakily recited the chant he had often used with his group. This time his voice echoed an empty sound throughout the large courtroom.

They continued in their most polished patterns, bringing out their best masks, their most rehearsed lies, their strongest defenses.

"I am the hero," said Kara. "I must find a way to save myself and my family from the shame. I have worked hard. I perform well. Surely I am better than the others, more deserving of being accepted as worthy."

"Why should I even try?" began Lisa in a whisper. "I am a poor, struggling single parent with no one to turn to, no one to care about me. I face everything alone. I never get a break. Why should you consider me now?"

"With a little 80 proof confidence I can come in here and be what I am not," declared Fred. "With a few more pills, I can numb the pain so that I don't even care what happens. It won't affect me. I don't have to mind the rules. I don't have to try. You can't fail if you don't try."

They continued in their most polished patterns, bringing out their best masks, their most rehearsed lies, their strongest defenses.

Their voices mingled, clamoring for attention, shouting, begging, pleading, intellectualizing, rationalizing, defending, blaming, shaming. . . . The uproar was intensified by a mechanical sound coming from overhead. Gradually the voices ceased. Only the noise of the mechanism remained. Eyes upward, all attention focused on a large object being lowered slowly from the ceiling.

It was a mirror. A plane mirror, a looking glass mirror, a biblical mirror: the mirror of The Law. Lisa, Fred, Kara, and Dick faced their reflections in the mirror of The Law. They were silent.

We are by nature and habit, by word and deed, WORTHLESS before God.

"'Whatever the law says, it says to those who are under the law, so that every mouth may be silenced'" (Romans 3:19), quoted the judge. "No more sniveling excuses, no more self-justifying rationalizations, no more self-destructive 'should haves,' no more shame-driven promises to do better. No more. Just 'shut up and listen' time."

The judge went on. "'Whatever the law says, it says to those who are under the law, so that . . . the whole world [is] held accountable to God' (Romans 3:19). Not some more than others; everyone accountable for everything to God. Not accountable to a demanding parent or an unreasonable boss or to an image of what you ought to be, but accountable to GOD. No comparisons with others; just one comparison—against the standard of holiness, the measure of perfection that is God."

"'Therefore, no one will be declared righteous in his sight by observing the law' (Romans 3:20). No matter how hard you try, no matter how much you do, it will never be enough to make the grade. Flawed from birth with a nature inclined to sin and failed from the first selfish inclination, NO ONE will pass muster with God on the basis of law. . . . NO ONE will receive the approval of 'righteous.' . . . NO ONE will find a reconciled relationship. The chase is futile, self-deluding, and self-destroying. God gave you his law to stop that chase."

The judge paused to allow the full impact of his words to sink in. Drawing a deep breath and softening his tone, he continued. "'Rather, through the law we become conscious of sin' (Romans 3:20). THAT is what the law is intended to do—afflict our conscience with the consciousness of sin, burst through the layers of deceit and confront us with the truth about ourselves, hold up a mirror so that we can see for ourselves THAT WE ARE SINNERS. Not little sinners or big sinners, just sinners. We are by nature and habit, by word and deed, WORTHLESS before God. That is the naked-truth reality. The law's purpose is to expose the total lack of moral worth in every human being, so that worth/identity can be found only in Jesus. Partial worth or comparative worth are deceptions responsible for the cycle of shame. Worthless in and of ourselves, we need to see the absolute worth God gives us."

"Are you saying that the specific sins and weaknesses of my human nature can be admitted, to myself and my God?" questioned Lisa. "And even beyond that, do you mean that I—like every other human being—am a sinner incapable of achieving SELF-worth and therefore misguided in seeking SELF-esteem?"

"I get it," said Dick slowly. "God's law exposes those sins and weaknesses, not so that I can work at self-improvement, but so that I can confess what is wrong with me."

"Only when I am emptied of tainted and artificial self-worth can I be filled with Christ's worth," reflected Fred.

"Only despairing of any self-righteousness can I be given Christ's righteousness," added Kara.

The judge summarized, "Instead of lies and half-truths about our identity, the law provides the truth about human nature's identity. That is its function as a MIRROR. We will see another mirror and a new identity tomorrow at 9 a.m. Court is adjourned for today."

In conclusion he rapped the gavel smartly on the desktop.

Instead of lies and half-truths about our identity, the law provides the truth about human nature's identity.

Reflections

1. Are you willing to look into the Biblical mirror of the law and see yourself as you are apart from God? Why? Why not?

2. How have you tried to cover up, deny, or atone for sin in your life?

3. Are you willing to admit that you are capable of the vilest of thoughts, the most cutting, piercing, and demeaning words, and the most heinous of acts against self, others, and God?

4. What specific shame must you admit to yourself and your God?

5. Who can help you be honest with yourself? Who will walk with you into God's presence with this burden of shame to unload?

CHAPTER 6

The Looking Glass—A Reflection of Christ

Mother stormed into the family room, where her four children were engrossed in a board game.

"All right, who ate the rest of the cookies when I said that there was to be no more snacking before supper?"

"Not I," came the familiar response from each child in turn.

"Not I," said Timmy, her six-year-old, averting his eyes as he wiped the tell-tale crumbs from his mouth.

"Then you will all have to go to your rooms until one of you comes forward and admits to eating the cookies," said Mother.

The children went to their respective rooms amid protests and complaining. Several minutes later, Timmy pattered down to the kitchen. Upon seeing her son, Mother sat down and gestured for him to sit on her lap. Head down, he approached her, and gingerly sat on one knee.

"I'm the one who ate the cookies," he finally blurted out. Stealing a quick glance at Mother, he saw the acceptance and love in her eyes. His large blue eyes welled up with tears. "Sorry," he said.

"Thank you for coming and telling me the truth. Please don't disobey me again." Timmy nodded. "Perhaps tomorrow you can help me bake another batch of cookies to share with the family."

He brightened. "That would be great."

Mother scooped her little boy into her arms. "I love you, Timmy," she said.

"I love you too, Mom."

Mother and child shared a big hug, a hug of confession, forgiveness, and restoration.

Plane mirrors: The biblical mirror of the gospel

What a relief it is to bring the truth to light! What a wonderful release there is in honest, sincere confession! It is like a breath of fresh air, a cleansing deep down inside, and a letting go of the burden of guilt and shame.

But that's not enough. What an overwhelming peace and security there is in knowing forgiveness, love, and restoration in response!

When we look into the biblical mirror of the law, we are silenced by the reality of our sin. We are guilty, guilty before our holy and righteous heavenly Father. Because he is also our loving and forgiving heavenly Father, we don't have to run away from him.

Instead, our sin drives us to our knees in honest confession. We can approach his heavenly throne in humble repentance; and he beckons us to come, sit upon his knee, and pour out our hearts to him.

Our sin drives us to our knees in honest confession.

Then, like children, we steal a glance at him and see the love and acceptance in his eyes.

We see a Father's love, unaltered by our disobedience, rebelliousness, and unworthiness: a love that culminated in its deepest expression on a cross, a love so giving that punished his own perfect Son in our place in order to save us, a love unconditional and everlasting. And our Father speaks hope, the good news of redemption and new life in Jesus Christ, his Son.

St. Paul writes in Romans 3, "But now a righteousness from God, apart from law, has been made known. . . . This righteousness from God comes through faith in Jesus Christ to all who believe. There is no difference, for all have sinned and fall short of the glory of God, and are justified freely by his grace through the redemption that came by Christ Jesus. God presented him as a sacrifice of atonement" (verses 21-25).

Our Father speaks hope, the good news of redemption and new life in Jesus Christ, his Son.

Two chapters later the apostle adds: "Just as the result of one trespass [Adam's] was condemnation for all men, so also the result of one act of righteousness [Jesus'] was justification that brings life for all men. For just as through the disobedience of the one man [Adam] the many were made sinners, so also through the obedience of the one man [Jesus] the many were made righteous" (5:18,19).

And in his second letter to the church at Corinth, Paul explains, "God was reconciling the world to himself in Christ, not counting men's sins against them. And he has committed to us the message of reconciliation. . . . God made him who had no sin to be sin for us, so that in him we might become the righteousness of God" (2 Corinthians 5:19-21).

Look into the mirror, the biblical mirror of the gospel.* The mirror image of Christ reflected in the gospel is your identity; it is my identity. It is our identity right now, and not anything or anyone can take it away from us.

It is God's gift to us, freely given by grace through faith.

Sin isn't overlooked or excused. It is punished and paid for. Jesus took the sin that was our heritage and identity, and he died for it. We got the righteousness that was Jesus' life and identity, and we live in it. The God who demands perfection has provided it for us in Christ.

In God's book, we are

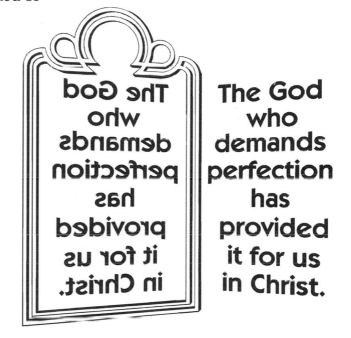

The God who demands perfection has provided it for us in Christ.

what Jesus was. That's our identity, the mirror image of the gospel.

Co-existing identities: Old sinful nature vs. new creations

Christians have two natures that are at war with each other. "The sinful nature desires what is contrary to the Spirit [describing the new life in Christ which the Holy Spirit has

---

*James 1:23-25 presents the metaphor of a "gospel mirror" in which we see our identity in Christ.

given Christians], and the Spirit what is contrary to the sinful nature. They are in conflict with each other, so that you do not do what you want" (Galatians 5:17).

Despite this conflict, our identity remains the same. God has declared us righteous in Christ, his children and heirs. The conflict remains through this life, but with St. Paul we can answer that cry: "Who will rescue me from this body of death? THANKS BE TO GOD—THROUGH JESUS CHRIST OUR LORD! . . . There is now no condemnation for those who are in Christ Jesus" (Romans 7:24—8:1).

Both biblical mirrors, law and gospel, are needed to show us our two natures. The law shows us our sinful nature, who we are apart from Christ— not so that we can make self-righteous corrections to become perfect, but, like little Timmy, daily to draw us near to our heavenly Father in confession and repentance. Then we turn to the gospel, which shows us who we are for Jesus' sake— redeemed, restored, perfect in Christ. We are reassured of our forgiveness and reconciliation with God. Our sins no longer are a barrier between us and our God.

> **Both biblical mirrors, law and gospel, are needed to show us our two natures.**

In Christ we are a "new creation," empowered to grow into the identity Christ has given us. Through God's Word, the Holy Spirit transforms us. Change in us is "inside out" as God convinces us of who we are in Christ. Not "living up to" requirements, but "living out" our identity in Christ describes the Christian's life. Therefore, St. Paul wrote: "Put off your old self, which is being corrupted by its deceitful desires; to be made new in the attitude of your minds; and to put on the new self, created to be like God in true righteousness and holiness" (Ephesians 4:22-24).

"I have been crucified with Christ and I no longer live, but Christ lives in me. The life I live in the body, I live by faith in the Son of God, who loved me and gave himself for me" (Galatians 2:20).

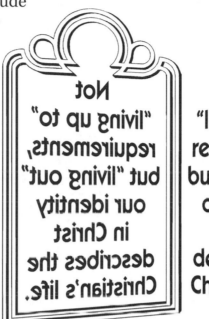

Not "living up to" requirements, but "living out" our identity in Christ describes the Christian's life.

Not one of the four had had a decent night's sleep. Dick, Kara, Lisa, and Fred shared their stories over coffee as they waited outside the court room doors: stories of restless tossing and turning, stories of late-night contemplation and thoughtfulness, stories of newly awakened excitement and hope.

They were ushered inside promptly at 9:00 a.m., with high anticipation.

The judge, after calling the session to order, informed them that each would be given a turn in the judge's chamber for individual reflection before the final verdict. He wished them well and disappeared through the back exit.

How God sees us for Jesus' sake

An attendant stood ready to escort the first participant to the chamber. Dick volunteered. The others watched as he was led away.

Alone in the room, Dick looked around. The room was serenely furnished with gentle colors and subdued lighting. He noted the mirror, a full-length dressing mirror in a corner of the room.

Dick purposely selected a chair away from the mirror and slipped into it. He sat tensely on the edge of the seat. He felt like a young boy, longing to approach his father, longing for his approval, but held at bay by a distant man who seemed impossible to please.

"I can never meet your standards, Lord," Dick began, "just as I could never meet the standards of my father. I learned that yesterday in the biblical mirror of the law.

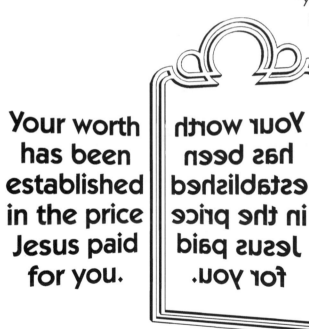

Your worth has been established in the price Jesus paid for you.

"You know I've tried. I've been driven to succeed, trying to prove to you that I can do it on my own, that I don't need you, that I don't care about you. But that isn't true.

"It's just that I've been so angry. I've thought of you as distant, judgmental, impersonal. I envisioned you laughing at my mistakes, dismissing me as too insig-nificant and weak to consider. Just like my earthly father.

"I'm so afraid to fail. I'm so afraid to admit to not being perfect. I'm so ashamed of failing you. Forgive me."

Pushing himself out of the chair, he stepped over to the gospel mirror. He stared into it.

Jesus returned his gaze—perfect, kind, forgiving, accepting. His arms were outstretched, hands still bearing the nail marks from his crucifixion.

A Father's voice said: "Dick, my son. You are fully pleasing to me. You need not struggle to attain perfection. It has already been attained for you by Jesus. You have been justified—declared righteous for the sake of Jesus' life and death in your place. Instead of the fear of failure, you have peace, hope, and joy through him. Your worth is not based on your success or failure. Your worth has been established in the price Jesus paid for you."

"Therefore, since we have been justified through faith, we have peace with God through our Lord Jesus Christ, through whom we have gained access by faith into this grace in which we now stand. And we rejoice in the hope of the glory of God" (Romans 5:1,2).

Kara felt the blood draining from her face as she numbly followed the attendant to the judge's chamber.

Once inside, she felt a touch of relief. At least the room seemed soothing, almost inviting. She noted the gospel mirror in the corner and began pacing along the other side of the room.

"I'm usually so poised, so controlled," she began. "I don't let my feelings out, never let anyone know I care.

"Remember, Lord, when Dad used to punish us kids? He'd get so out of control, yelling, ranting and raving, lashing out. I was the only one who wouldn't say a word. I wasn't going to let him know that he could get to me.

"I worked so hard, and it was never enough. No mention was ever made of positives or successes. But we sure heard about every little mistake, every failure, every imperfection.

"I've gotten quite good at covering my mistakes, using positions of authority to blame and punish others, and avoid scrutiny myself. It doesn't work with you, does it. Lord? I learned that yesterday.

"I feel so worthless inside, and so alone. I've withdrawn from you, God, and from others. I want to come close, but I'm so afraid that you will punish me, too."

She slowly edged over to the biblical mirror of the gospel and took a careful look.

There was her Savior. She remembered the pain he endured, the suffering, the agony, the judgment, the punishment—unfair, unjust, endured out of love for her. But it was the perfect, risen, and glorious Savior who looked back at her from the mirror.

"Kara, my daughter," came the voice of her heavenly Father, reaching out to her through the arms of his Son. "I have poured out my righteous anger upon my Son on the cross. I judged him with the punishment that you deserved. Jesus Christ, your Savior, satisfied my holy demands with his life, and my righteous justice with his death.

"My love for you does not change, whether you achieve, succeed, fail, or stumble.

"My love for you does not change, whether you achieve, succeed, fail, or stumble. It is unconditional and everlasting.

"I love you. I love you, my little Kara. I will always love you."

"This is how God showed his love among us: He sent his one and only Son into the world that we might live through him. This is love: not that we loved God, but that he loved us and sent his Son as an atoning sacrifice for our sins" (1 John 4:9,10).

Fred hurried down the hall after the attendant. Upon reaching the door, he hesitated. He had faced a lot of rejection in his lifetime. Could this possibly be different?

"Only one way to find out," he said to himself as he marched through the door.

He came to an abrupt halt upon seeing the mirror. Shoving his hands into his pockets, he looked down at the floor.

"Hey, I don't pretend to be some kind of likable guy," he began. "I know I'm rebellious, a trouble-maker, and a wise-guy.

"My parents didn't like me; my teachers didn't like me. My siblings and peers made fun of me. Nobody thought I was worth much. I've never been able to do anything right, so why try? Right? I know—not right. I saw that in the other mirror we looked at yesterday.

"I've always wanted to be accepted, to feel like I belong. That's why, I guess, I've tried to fit in with the deviant crowd. I know I'd never make it with those goody-goodies. How can I ever make it with you?"

Let my love
for you
heal the pain
of rejection
you have
experienced.

Fred raised his eyes and studied the mirror. He found himself transfixed by the overwhelming acceptance that he saw in his Savior's eyes.

It was as though his heavenly Father called to him through the love emanating from his Son. "Fred, my son, you are fully acceptable in my sight. When I look at you now, I see my Son. He was right—in your place—where you've been wrong. He atoned for everything you've done wrong. Jesus reconciled you back to me. You need never fear my rejection. Let my love for you heal the pain of rejection you have experienced. Be happy. You are mine."

"Once you were alienated from God and were enemies in your minds because of your evil behavior. But now he has reconciled you by Christ's physical body through death to present you holy in his sight, without blemish and free from accusation" (Colossians 1:21,22).

At last it was Lisa's turn. She followed hesitantly as the attendant took her to the judge's chamber. Slowly she entered the room.

"What a lovely room," she thought in surprise. "So peaceful, so tranquil." Gratefully she sank into a chair and quietly studied the room.

It reminded her of her room as a child. That room had been her "safe place," her haven from the storms around her. She had spent countless hours there, playing, imagining, pretending.

"I used to pretend that I was someone else, anyone but me would do. It was my escape from the loneliness, the frightening, hurtful world outside. Plus, I didn't like my real self very well. I guess that I really didn't even know who I was.

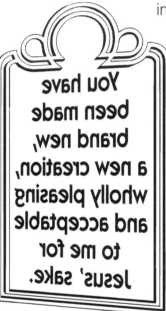

You have been made brand new, a new creation, wholly pleasing and acceptable to me for Jesus' sake.

"My opinions, thoughts, wants, feelings, needs didn't seem to matter much to anyone else. I experienced the same thing at school—feeling inferior, hopeless, shamed, side-lined. Such a lonely place to be.

"I've always wondered about you, God. Whether you were there watching me, whether you cared. I sort of thought you did, but I was too afraid to find out for certain. I didn't consider myself worth your time."

Tears, which seemed to come more often than not, slowly slid down her cheeks. Brushing them aside, she stood, and approached the mirror. Peering into the reflecting surface, her heart jumped in longing recognition of the love, acceptance, and specialness that she had always dreamed of. It wasn't Lisa in the mirror—that Lisa she'd always apologized for and regretted. Her beautiful, loving Savior reached out to her in welcome, drawing her toward him and giving her HIS identity.

The words of her heavenly Father filled her mind in blessing. "Lisa, my daughter, how I have longed to draw you close to me. How I have longed to show you how special and complete you are in Christ. You have been made brand new, a new creation, wholly pleasing and acceptable to me for Jesus' sake. Let all shame and sadness go. Get on with life in joy, courage, and peace. Be filled with Christ-centered confidence. 'For I know the plans I have for you. Plans to prosper you and not to harm you, plans to give you hope and a future.'" Jer. 29:11

"Therefore, if anyone is in Christ, he is a new creation; the old has gone, the new has come!" (2 Corinthians 5:17).

Rapha, in its 12-step programs for co-dependency and chemical dependency, summarizes God's specific solutions to the four false beliefs discussed in Chapter 5:

God's specific solution		Result of God's solution
Because of justification, we are completely forgiven and fully pleasing to God. We no longer have to fear failure.		Increasing freedom from the fear of failure; desire to pursue the right things: Christ and his kingdom; love for Christ.
Because of reconciliation, we are totally accepted by God. We no longer have to fear rejection.		Increasing freedom from the fear of rejection; willingness to be open and vulnerable; able to relax around others; willingness to take

God's specific solution	Result of God's solution
	criticism; desire to please God, no matter what others think.
Because of propitiation, we have the capacity to experience God's love deeply. We no longer have to fear punishment or punish others. →	Increasing freedom from the fear of punishment; patience and kindness toward others; being quick to forgive; deep love for Christ.
Because of regeneration, we have been made brand new, complete in Christ. We no longer need to experience the pain of shame. →	Christ-centered self-confidence; joy, courage, peace; desire to know Christ better.

*

REFLECTIONS

1. What, specifically, do you appreciate about Jesus as you see yourself given HIS identity?

2. What Bible study opportunities will you take advantage of in order to better know, accept, and personalize God's forgiving love?

---

*McGee, Robert S., Springle, Pat, and Joiner, Susan, *Rapha's Twelve-Step Program for Overcoming Chemical Dependency*, Rapha Publishing / Word Inc., Houston and Dallas, Texas, 1990. Reprinted by permission.

3. Imagine God's individual response to you as you sit upon his knee and pour out to him all those things that you have kept hidden inside.

4. What does your heavenly Father say to you?

CHAPTER 7

Reflecting on the Trinity— Our Passport to Identity

We have faced the judge. The moment from which we have squirmed away, as a termite scrambles from light, has arrived. We cowered, we cringed, desperate to hide our deadly secret. But the law exposed us—exposed us for what we are—sinners. We know the sentence we deserve—GUILTY—condemned for all eternity.

The verdict rings in our ears: JUSTIFIED—NOT GUILTY—RIGHTEOUS. Why? For the sake of Jesus Christ, our Savior. What joy! What relief! What hope! Our eyes turn back to God, and we see him as we have never seen him before—love incomprehensible and unmerited, amazing grace, mercy without measure. The gospel trumpets God's Great Exchange.

Through faith in Jesus, we have a new identity.

Our heavenly Father prosecuted his one and only Son in our place. God exchanged the perfection of Jesus for our sin. He who achieved the perfection we couldn't, suffered the death penalty we deserved. Jesus got our sin and died under it. We got the righteousness of Jesus and live with God in it. The resurrection of Jesus was God's seal on this exchange, and the beginning of our hope.

Through faith in Jesus we have a new identity. "Therefore, if anyone is in Christ, he is a new creation; the old has gone, the new has come!" (2 Corinthians 5:17). Let us discover all that we can about our new identity.

UNDERSTANDING SELF BY REFLECTING ON GOD
God the Father: Father, Foreman, Friend
Father

Father—we can call him that now. "Our Father who art in heaven . . ." He is our Father by creation. But sin wrenched us out of his loving arms. How much more is he our Father by redemption, adopting us back into his family at the price of his Son Jesus!

He provides us with the family we have always longed for, one filled with security, belonging, and roots—a basis for our identity. He surrounds us with total acceptance and unconditional love. Our human families will remain imperfect, sometimes filled with pain and

Our heavenly Father is waiting for us, with love in his eyes and his arms wide open.

scars that only he can heal. But always we are at home in his family.

Like the Prodigal Son of Jesus' parable, we are all prodigals in one way or another. The world pulls, attracts, and tempts, promising what it can't deliver, offering treasures and pleasures that glitter, then tarnish.

Isn't it time to go home? Our heavenly Father is waiting for us, with love in his eyes and his arms open wide. He offers complete forgiveness, absolute acceptance.

"Let's have a feast and celebrate. For this son of mine was dead and is alive again; he was lost and is found" (Luke 15:23,24).

Foreman

We try so hard to stay in control. We figure all the angles, plot and plan. We direct events and manage people. We calculate, dictate, orchestrate, regulate, manipulate, and officiate life and everyone in it. Are you out of breath yet? Stop for just a minute. Take a deep breath and face the facts: We are not in control; God is! He is the foreman, and he calls the shots. Things aren't out of control. He is in control. We

HIS will!
HIS kingdom!
HIS power!
HIS glory!
Not ours.

may see only loose ends. He makes connections. We worry short-term. He plans long-run. We wonder about brush strokes. He paints the big picture in great detail. And he painted us into his picture.

St. Paul draws the obvious conclusion: "In all things God works for the good of those who love him, who have been called according to his purpose. . . . If God is for us, who can be against us? He who did not spare his own Son but gave him up for us all—how will he not also, along with [Jesus], graciously give us all things?" (Romans 8:28-32).

HIS will! HIS kingdom! HIS power! HIS glory! Not ours. Our role as believers is to get out of the way, let go and let God.

Friend

God wants to be our dear friend. The lines of communication have been opened through our Savior. We can go to him directly, any time, any place.

What do we want to do most with our friends? Spend time with them! We write that time into the calendar. We make a list of all the things we want to talk about. We collect little things we want to share: pictures, mementoes, a devotion or poem, that new book we just finished reading. We can hardly wait to get together to pour out our hearts to someone who understands, accepts us as we are, and loves us anyway.

First and foremost, Jesus is our Savior.

That's how God wants it to be for us with him. He's looking forward to that fellowship time we need to write into our busy schedules. He wants us to pour our hearts out to him, to share all that is on our minds. He has so much to tell us: the plans he has for us, the identity he is bringing out in us, his truth to counter our lies, his strength in our weakness, and the constant assurance of his great love for us.

"Your hand will guide me," the psalmist says to the Lord, "For you created my inmost being. . . . How precious to me are your thoughts, O God! . . . Search me . . . and know my heart" (Psalm 139:10,13,17,23).

God the Son: Savior, Substitute, Sibling, Servant

Savior

First and foremost, Jesus is our Savior. Our whole identity depends on that fact. He lived and died to save us from what we did to ourselves. He rose again to tell us what he's done for us.

Substitute

We can trade in the mask of perfection for the real thing. God the Son has given us HIS perfection. His Father has declared us perfect— righteous—for Jesus' sake. We can let go of perfectionism because Jesus has taken the punishment for all our imperfections and has given us his perfection in exchange. "By one sacrifice he has made perfect forever those who are being made holy" (Hebrews 10:14).

That passage presents the paradox of Christian life. While we are "perfect forever" in Christ, we are "being made holy" in a life of growing obedience to our Lord. St. Paul says it this way: "Not that I have already . . . been made perfect, but I press on to take hold of that for which Christ Jesus took hold of me" (Philippians 3:12). We are growing into an identity that we already have.

Sibling

Not only have we gained a heavenly Father, but we've gained a Big Brother as well. In Jesus we have the Big Brother that we always wanted—someone to look up to, someone we want to be just like, someone to protect us and teach us, someone to be there in life's rough spots, someone who understands and who cares. "We have a great high priest who has gone through the heavens, Jesus the Son of God. . . . We do not have a high priest who is unable to sympathize with our weaknesses, but we have one who has been tempted in every way, just as we are—yet was without sin. Let us then approach the throne of grace with confidence, so that we may receive mercy and find grace to help us in our time of need" (Hebrews 4:14-16).

Our Big Brother enables us to admit what's wrong with us, confide our hurts, share our

The life that Jesus models is in sharp contrast to worldly attitudes and behavior.

questions, be ourselves. We don't have to be something more. He has made us all there could ever be.

Servant

We are imitators of Jesus. He is our role model. It is into his identity that we wish to grow.

Growing up, we wonder what is normal, acceptable behavior. We look to parents, teachers, older siblings, and peers to show us what to be. We observe models in television, literature, advertising. All too often we get conflicting messages and unhealthy role models. Some tell us, "Do as I say, not as I do." Others are doing AND saying what will only get us hurt.

The life that Jesus models is in sharp contrast to worldly attitudes and behavior. The account of Jesus washing his disciples' feet begins: "Jesus knew that the Father had put all things under his power and that he had come from God and was returning to God; [SO] he got up from the meal, took off his outer clothing, and wrapped a towel around his waist" (John 13:3,4). Jesus knew who he was. He didn't have anything to prove. SO he could wash feet. The disciples were insecure, seeking approval and position. They wouldn't wash feet for fear that it would be taken as a statement about their worth, their place in the pecking order. "Your attitude," St. Paul writes, "should be the same as that of Christ Jesus: Who, being in very nature God, did not consider equality with God something to be grasped, but made himself nothing, taking the very nature of a servant" (Philippians 2:5).

False humility, pretending to be less than we are, is a mask that only true humility can strip away. Deflation, self-hatred in disguise, won't be resolved with pep talks about self-esteem and props of personal worth. Take a close look at Jesus, the one who was everything and made himself nothing, the model of true humility.

True humility is knowing that in Christ you are everything you could ever be, have everything there is worth having. You have nothing to prove, nowhere to climb. From that position of strength you, like your Savior, can find great joy in serving.

God the Holy Spirit: Counselor, Character-builder

Counselor

Jesus called the Holy Spirit the COUNSELOR. He's the one who applies all that Jesus has done, all the Father has said, to our hearts and lives. He offers truth's "objective viewpoint" when we're too emotionally involved in a situation to see clearly. When we attempt denial, stonewall God, and don the mask of perfectionism, the Holy Spirit cuts through all the lies and confronts us with our sin. When we rationalize and excuse ourselves, blaming others and minimizing our faults, the Holy Spirit challenges the lies so that—like David—we confess: "Against you, you only, have I sinned and done what is evil in your sight, so that you are proved right when you speak and justified when you judge" (Psalm 51:4).

He does not leave us distressed. He personalizes the forgiveness Jesus died to earn, and reminds us of the identity our baptism gave us. He renews hope and restores confidence, applying to our hearts and situations the Word of God that is "a lamp to my feet and a light for my path" (Psalm 119:105). Jesus said, "But when he, the Spirit of truth, comes, he will guide you into all truth" (John 16:13).

He's the one who applies all that Jesus has done, all the Father has said, to our hearts and lives.

Martin Luther, in his hymn "Come, Holy Spirit," prays:

Thou holy Light, Guide Divine,
Oh, cause the Word of Life to shine!
Teach us to know our God aright
And call Him Father with delight.
From every error keep us free;
Let none but Christ our Master be
That we in living faith abide,
In Him, our Lord, with all our might confide. Hallelujah!

Thou holy Fire, Comfort true,
Grant us the will Thy work to do
And in Thy service to abide;
Let trials turn us not aside.
Lord, by Thy power prepare each heart
And to our weakness strength impart,
That bravely here we may contend,
Through life and death to Thee, our God, ascend. Hallelujah!

Character-builder

Each of us has significance —a role to play and a gift to share.

Are we really good for anything, important to anybody, or are we as worthless as we sometimes feel? The Holy Spirit has the answer for us. "In Christ we who are many form one body, and each member belongs to all the others. We have different gifts, according to the grace given us" (Romans 12:5,6). The Holy Spirit unites us with other Christians. We need each other, and as a body we cannot function properly unless all our parts are in good working order. God "needs" us, to be his hands and voices, extensions of his love.

Each of us has significance—a role to play and a gift to share. "Spiritual gifts" is the Bible's term for the special abilities the Holy Spirit gives Christians to accomplish the mission of Christ and his church. Some of us have gifts that put us out front. Others blend easily into the background, often go unnoticed, but are no less significant.

We recently installed an underground sprinkler system. It was fascinating to watch as the workers mapped out the path it would take, laid piping and sprinkler heads, then rigged up a pump and hose combination to draw water from our pond. There were many different components that went into the system. When we turned it on for the first time, we held our breath as the pump drew the water from the pond through the hose and sent it through the underground pipes where the water pressure forced the sprinkler heads out of the ground with a glorious spray of water fireworks. Connected to the Source, with all components working together, we are—together—the Holy Spirit's glorious system for distributing the water of life.

The Holy Spirit changes us, making us more like Christ.

The Holy Spirit uses our life experiences to build character. The trials we face are God's tools of character-building. The challenges are opportunities to grow. We become able to "rejoice in our sufferings, because we know that suffering produces perseverance; perseverance, character; and character, hope. And hope does not disappoint us, because God has poured out his love into our hearts by the Holy Spirit, whom he has given us" (Romans 5:3-5).

The Holy Spirit changes us, making us more like Christ. We see what St. Paul called "fruit of the Spirit" growing in our lives. We see love where there was spite, joy where there was bitterness, peace where there was anxiety, patience where there was self-will, kindness where there was malice, goodness where there was evil, faithfulness where there was betrayal, gentleness where there was harshness, and self-control where there was self-indulgence.

God is faithful. "He who began a good work in you will carry it on to completion until the day of Christ Jesus" (Philippians 1:6). The Holy Spirit wants to make more of our lives here and now, all the while assuring us that Jesus has made our lives everything they could be forever.

Reflections

1. Agree/Disagree: Though the Prodigal Son of Jesus' parable didn't want to be his father's son and later believed he'd forfeited the right to be his father's son, he never stopped being his father's son.

   What are the implications of your answer for your own life?

2. What sins have you been unwilling to let Jesus take to the cross and bury? What hurts and weaknesses have you been hanging onto instead of releasing them to God in prayer?

3. Read Psalm 22, a prophecy of Christ's passion. (Verses 14-18 can only be speaking of Christ at the cross.) Verse one is David's cry and, in fulfillment, Christ's cry as he endured God's punishment for our sin. Have you felt like crying out these same words? Do you feel closer to Jesus knowing how fully he experienced what you do, and how fully he has suffered for you? How many similar emotions, shared by Jesus, do you see in Psalm 22?

4. How do each of the Persons of the Trinity change your image of yourself?

5. For what gifts in your character can you thank the Lord right now?

CHAPTER 8

Repentance/ Renewal— A New Cycle with God

"Surely you desire truth in the inner parts; you teach me wisdom in the inmost place" (Psalm 51:6).

God desires truth in the inner parts. He is not talking about looking good on the outside. The light of his truth exposes the deepest crevices of our being, all the corners, closets, and hiding places we have inside.

Human nature wants to hold on to pet sins, unwilling to acknowledge them before God.

Human nature wants to hold on to pet sins, unwilling to acknowledge them before God. Bitterness and resentment burrow deep inside. We cling to that addiction, foster those impure thoughts, harbor unforgiveness and self-pity. We rationalize: "I only did it once."

"It doesn't hurt anybody else."

"It's nothing compared to what others do."

We bargain, thinking that there must be something we can do to appease God and earn his favor. Only when God has exposed our lies can he heal us with his forgiving love.

Good Housekeeping

Lord, it is not the dirt and clutter in plain sight
    that nag at me.
It's that hidden dirt . . . you know, behind the
    refrigerator, in the closets, under the bed.
Dirt that no one sees or knows about but me.
It's the same way with my life, God.
It's those hidden sins that I can't keep up with . . . those
    petty little grievances, the grudges,
    the resentments, the unspoken harsh feelings,
    the superior attitudes.
Thoughts and feelings, that no one else knows about but
    me . . . and You, God.
Help me, Father, to clean my heart as I would my home.
Take away all dust and cobwebs of pride, ill feelings and
    prejudice .
The dirt behind my refrigerator will never hurt anyone.
The dirt in my heart will.

Source Unknown

Recognize, repent, request

Recognize

"For I know my transgressions, and my sin is always before me. Against you, you only, have I sinned and done what is evil in your sight, so that you are proved right when you speak and justified when you judge. Surely I was sinful at birth, sinful from the time my mother conceived me" (Psalm 51:3-5).

We *are* sinful from birth. And that sinful human nature leaves footprints on each day of our lives. It is essential that we daily take stock of our lives, search out and recognize our sin. Don't hold back. Let ALL the guilt come out. Lay ALL the sins on the table before God. Challenge the lingering doubt that God will really forgive all those sins, that some must remain hidden in the recesses of your conscience because they are too awful to face. God already knows them all. Jesus already died for them all. We want the cleansed conscience of a complete forgiveness.

The Holy Spirit won't let us rest in our sins. Through God's commands, he arouses our awareness of sin. We hear that inner voice of conscience prodding, provoking, pressing. It's always there, nagging at us, intruding on our thoughts, robbing us of any real sense of well-being. We just have to be rid of it. More than this, however, sin is the wedge between us and our God. It leaves us somewhere between afraid and embarrassed to come to him. We know we've offended him; and we can't rest until this has been resolved.

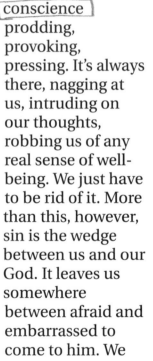

Sinful human nature leaves footprints on each day of our lives.

Recognition is dropping all the rationalizations and acknowledging that sin is against GOD, whether anyone else gets hurt or not, whether we do it more than once or not. God has a right to judge and is right when he condemns sin.

Recognition is admitting that sin isn't simply what's wrong with what I did, but what's wrong with me. Human nature, what we are by birth (without rebirth in Christ), is totally corrupt and incapable of ever getting life right.

Repent

"Have mercy on me, O God, according to your unfailing love; according to your great compassion blot out my transgressions. Wash away all my iniquity and cleanse me from my sin" (Psalm 51:1,2). → *A repentence psalm*

"The sacrifices of God are a broken spirit; a broken and contrite heart, O God, you will not despise" (Psalm 51:17).

The repentant attitude is a broken spirit and a contrite heart. We leave the masks and cover-ups behind in order simply to be ourselves. We are stripped of all that we think of ourselves, stripped of all that friends or relatives say of us. We stand in naked honesty before God, "Just as I am."

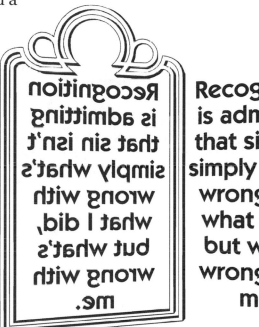

Recognition is admitting that sin isn't simply what's wrong with what I did, but what's wrong with me.

We come as children, certain of a Father's love. We will not come if we don't know him as our Father, if we forget the proof of his love in the death of his Son. We will not come if we are still denying or defying God. Repentance begins with an attitude of humble trust.

Faith turns mere sorrow over sin into repentance, faith that God both can and will take away our sin, faith based on the simple truth that Jesus died for MY sin. Faith prompts the prayer that God will lift the crushing weight of guilt that has depressed a person's spirit and robbed the Christian's joy. It is the confident prayer that God will forget what he forgives, blot sin out of the record and no longer see it when he looks at his dear child. Repentance is asking for forgiveness and knowing that, for Jesus' sake, the petition is answered.

Request

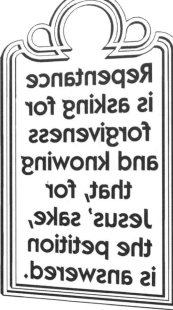

> "Cleanse me with hyssop, and I will be clean; wash me, and I will be whiter than snow. Let me hear joy and gladness; let the bones you have crushed rejoice. Hide your face from my sins and blot out all my iniquity" (Psalm 51:7-9).

From this vulnerable position, what is it we most long for? We want to be washed. We want to be made clean, a deep-down clean that leaves us "whiter than snow." We can just feel all the grime of sin being wiped away, all the weight of guilt and baggage of shame removed. We want cobwebs gone from our thinking, the film wiped from our eyes, and no more wax plugging our ears. Once again we want to hear the joy and gladness of God's voice assuring us that he's forgiven us, loves us, and will one day take us to be with him. We want the happiness only God can give us.

Renewal: God's response

God CAREs. He hears us and responds. We repent, God renews. Out of his love and CARE for us, God does what Psalm 51 prays: Creates, Accepts, Restores, Elicits—

C: Creates in us a pure heart and renews a steadfast spirit within us. (cf. Psalm 51:10)

Renewal begins with a new heart and mind that sees life God's way and wants what God wills. St. Paul describes the process this way: "Do not conform any longer to the pattern of this world, but be transformed by the renewing of your mind. Then you will be able to test and approve what God's will is—his good, pleasing and perfect will" (Romans 12:2). God's Word renews our minds, straightening out warped thinking, reshaping values and attitudes, redirecting life.

We want the happiness only God can give us.

A: Accepts us and fills us with his Holy Spirit. (cf. Psalm 51:11)

God accepts us totally for Jesus' sake, gives us access to him now in prayer, and promises the full enjoyment of his presence forever. He fills us with his Holy Spirit, who accomplishes renewal in us through the Word. Through that Word of God, the Spirit renews our trust in Jesus, our desire to serve him, our strength to do so. Time with our Bibles is vital to the renewal we so desperately want.

R: Restores to us the joy of His salvation and grants us a willing spirit, to sustain us. (Psalm 51:12).

Renewal is getting our joy back. Real joy—joy that is not simply happiness with one's circumstance nor a mere experience of the senses. Joy is the "joy of your salvation," knowing that we are OK because God has said so, knowing that our life is OK because God is watching over it, and knowing that "all is well with my soul" because God's plan of salvation is fulfilled. "The joy of the Lord is [my] strength" (Nehemiah 8:10).

E: Elicits a response from us.

Gratitude to God for salvation, coupled with joy in being God's saved child, provides the will to serve.

Time with our Bibles is vital to the renewal we so desperately want.

WITNESS: "Then I will teach transgressors your ways, and sinners will turn back to you" (Psalm 51:13).

WORSHIP: "Save me from bloodguilt, O God, the God who saves me, and my tongue will sing of your righteousness. O Lord, open my lips, and my mouth will declare your praise" (Psalm 51:14,15).

Witness to the lost . . . admonition, encouragement to other sinners . . . praise and testimony to our gracious God—that is what renewal does to a Christian's life. It is getting back our purpose and discovering how much joy there is in fulfilling that purpose.

Every day we can cleanse and renew our lives, reclaim our identity and status as God's dear children, rediscover all the implications of that identity in our thoughts and feelings, redirect our lives with God's will and power. God's grace invites us. God's Word works in us.

A. W. Tozer offers the following prayer in his book, *The Pursuit of God:*

> Lord, I would trust Thee completely; I would be altogether Thine; I would exalt Thee above all. I desire that I may feel no sense of possessing anything outside of Thee. I want constantly to be aware of Thy overshadowing Presence and to hear Thy speaking Voice. I long to live in restful sincerity of heart. I want to live so fully in the Spirit that all my thought may be as sweet incense ascending to Thee and every act of my life may be an act of worship. Therefore I pray in the words of Thy great servant of old, 'I beseech Thee so to cleanse the intent of mine heart with the unspeakable gift of Thy grace, that I may perfectly love Thee and worthily praise Thee.' And all this I confidently believe Thou wilt grant me through the merits of Jesus Christ Thy Son. Amen.   (p. 128.)

Reflections

1. Read Psalm 32 and jot down elements of the REPEN-TANCE/ RENEWAL cycle that are the same as outlined in Psalm 51.

God's grace invites us. God's Word works in us.

2. Think through the

patterns of your normal day. Where, in each day, should you schedule time out for Scripture and prayer to interrupt the negative cycle of shame and replace it with repentance and renewal?

3. Call your church and enroll in a Bible class that will rebuild your understanding of your God, yourself, and your life, and reconnect you to brothers and sisters in Christ.

4. Identify one thing that you can do to serve your God with the gifts he has given you; and use that purposeful service to replace a negative pattern in your life.